CW00970834

Daytrading for beginners

The most important basics and lessons for successful daytraders.

Jordan Kingsford

1st edition

2020

ISBN: 978-3-949256-04-2

Table of contents

First Steps

Before we begin, I would like to thank you for taking the time to read my book. I am glad that you took the trouble to learn more about day trading, a fascinating but often misunderstood way of making money.

Be prepared to learn a lot of information in a short time. I have included explanations and definitions of terms you may not be familiar with in the book itself.

In this book I will show you how to set up an account and a "home office" and how to use specialized tools to make your first trade. This is the easy part.

The difficult part is to use all this information to increase earnings. Although you are about to embark on an educational and enjoyable journey, my ultimate goal is to teach you how to become a better trader while helping you manage your risk.

And now let's get started!

What is day trading?

"Day trading" or "intra-day trading" is a method that works exactly the way it sounds: You enter a trade in one or more shares (or another security) and leave the trade - which you only held on to for seconds, minutes or hours - at the end of the day.

It's just semantics, but in this book I often refer to daytrading as a strategy. You could also call it a technique, a style or an activity. The goal is to make a trade and get out at a profit - the sooner the better - and still sleep well.

Although the content of this book was written with the DACH and US stock markets in mind, the information contained in this book can be applied to any stock market in which you trade.

Myths vs. reality

There are many myths about "day trading". Since uninformed traders have made mistakes in the past, many people think that day trading is too risky. They mistakenly believe that "day traders" are chained in front of a computer for ten hours a day, making hundreds of lightning-fast trades and stealing pennies worth 500 Euros. Although a handful of people may fit this stereotype, many modern day traders are more selective about the deals they make.

They tend to act more intelligently and make only a handful of transactions per day. Rather than being very active traders (making hundreds of trades per day), some day traders prefer to be high probability traders (trading when the odds are in their favor).

It is really a personal decision what kind of dealer you will be. "Daytrading" does not mean that you can lounge around in front of a pool in Bali while trading with a laptop or cell phone. Although some lax traders have made transactions during their never-ending vacation, it is unlikely that they will be profitable in this environment for long.

Why not? Most day traders need to focus on their screen like a laser beam with no distractions; they need to be alert and up to date. Dealers work very hard - you can schedule fifty to sixty hour work weeks.

They are also responsible for their own taxes, technical support and training. They have to make lightning-fast decisions, and if they are wrong, it could cost them money. Without a regular paycheck, many traders face enormous pressure to overtrade in order to make money. As markets are constantly changing, traders must also constantly evolve and adapt to market conditions.

A strategy that works well one year may not work the next year. Even with all these challenges, it is possible to be a successful "day trader", but you have to work hard. On the positive side, this also means that you have your time and schedule under control.

You do not have to commute to an office and report to a boss. It is extremely satisfying to find a good deal and be rewarded with money. And remember, you can trade from anywhere in the world, there is no dress code, and you have the freedom to set your own financial goals.

Some traders have combined the best of both worlds by trading part-time. For example, you could initiate a trade in the morning and set up automatic triggers to sell when the stock reaches a certain price. In this case, day trading is simply another strategy that is used when market conditions are right. In the next chapter you will learn more about the advantages of part-time trading.

Why should you read this book ?

If you are a newcomer among traders and would like to learn more about "day trading", you have come to the right place.

You will learn how to integrate "day trading strategies" into your trading portfolio. And if you are thinking of becoming a "full-time day trader", after reading this book you will have a better idea of whether "day trading" is for you.

No matter what kind of trader you are, many of the lessons you will learn in this book will be invaluable. I will also help you avoid some of the most common trading pitfalls.

If you are reading this book out of curiosity or for entertainment, I will do my best to meet your needs. Like all my other books, I try to explain "day trading" as if you were sitting across from me at my kitchen table. My goal is to save you time and money while teaching and keeping you busy.

You will learn:

- How to get started, including how much money you will need, how to select and use a broker and how to set up a trading account.

- How to read "charts" - an indispensable tool for "day traders".

- How to use technical indicators to determine where the market or an individual stock is going.

- How to make a trade - I will guide you step by step through your first trading day.

- How you deal with your money and emotions.

- And much more...

How much money can I earn?

You probably want to know how much money you can earn as a "Day Trader". Maybe you have even set yourself a goal - for example 200 to 300 € per day. The desire to make money may even be the reason why you are reading this book.

Let me tell you the first goal of this book:

It should help you to act well. Although making profits is a worthwhile long-term goal, it is secondary to trading with the odds in your favor and the probabilities. **Instead of asking "How much money can I make", the first question you should ask is "How much money can I lose? Your financial security is my most important concern, a responsibility I take very seriously.** You can only earn money if you act correctly every day.

If you don't, you could lose all your money faster than you can say, "What happened? If you want to do "day trading", you need to be aware of both the risks and the benefits. **Too many people enter the market with too much money and too little knowledge.** In fact, one of the reasons that "day trading" has a bad reputation is that thousands of people have quit their full-time jobs, cashed in their 401(k) accounts and dumped everything into the market. Many "day traders" achieved extraordinary returns, especially at the top of a bull market. Unfortunately, bull markets do not last forever. If they end abruptly, many once successful strategies stop working and people lose money. Unfortunately, they sometimes lose more than what they started with.

Remember that:

If you learn to act well, you can act for a lifetime, not just for one day. **Therefore, while reading this book, focus on**

being the best trader you can be. When you finish reading, you will not only learn how to do "day trading", but also whether "day trading" makes sense for you and your financial goals.

Earn 1.000 € per day

I will tell you a short anecdote: I have a girlfriend who was fascinated by how I could enter the market and pull money out seemingly effortlessly.

She assumed that the stock market was a giant ATM machine. Once she called me and said: "I need 1,000 euros. Could you make a trade for me?" This reminded me of the nightly commercials that promised "1,000 € a day if you work from the comfort of your own home! Nevertheless, it is possible to consistently earn 1,000 € per day, but hardly likely, even if you have a 100,000 € account. Even 500 € per day, or 0.5 percent, would be fantastic.

Thousands of professional fund managers would do anything to achieve this kind of return. My suggestion is to learn about daily trading without setting daily financial goals. Start by gathering knowledge and experience. Over time, you will discover that the key to your success is discipline, a characteristic we will discuss in detail in this book.

The biggest obstacle to your success

Many large institutions spend hundreds of millions of dollars on high-speed computers and complex algorithms to make thousands or more trades per day, giving them a penny advantage over other traders. These pennies add up to billions of euros per year. With so many institutions using these high frequency strategies, day trading has become more competitive than ever.

Fortunately the lonely "daytrader" can flourish. Although it is not as easy as some people hope, "daytrading" is also not as risky as many people think. If you learn to overcome the biggest obstacle on the way to your success, you can conquer a profitable niche.

This obstacle? Your emotions.

Learning how to do "day trading" is the easy part. The difficult part is overcoming the psychological challenges. I dedicate a chapter to this topic, but it could take some time before you learn to ignore your instincts and control your emotions. If there is anything that can harm your account, it is your emotions.

Now that you have a more realistic idea of what you are dealing with, let's get started. Remember that **with the right information, tools and mental attitude you can be a successful "daytrader".**

Chapter 1: Learning the business

In this chapter you will learn how to open a broker account, understand the capital requirements and set up your "home office". You will also learn basic trading information and terminology.

Selection of a brokerage house

Once you have decided to trade on a daily basis, you must choose a brokerage firm that is a registered stock broker that acts as an intermediary between buyers and sellers. You will need to open an account with a brokerage firm to buy or sell shares. This important decision requires careful research.

Brokerage firms can be divided into three main types (and all of them have sophisticated trading platforms and online access):

- Online discount brokers are for self-directed traders, they offer little or no investment advice, low commissions, fast, sophisticated options, independence and customer service.

- Brokerage firms with direct access are similar to online discount brokers, but are usually geared towards the professional trader, offering little support for beginners, and low execution, charting and research commissions for high-volume traders.

- "Full-service brokerage firms" work primarily with long-term investors and not with day traders. You instruct them to work with a stockbroker's representative for an annual fee or a costly commission, i.e. the price you pay for investment advice and stock ideas.

Selection of an online broker

When you choose an online trading brokerage firm, choose one that has a nationally recognized reputation, 12-hour support to answer questions, and competitive commissions (less than $10 per trade).

For inexperienced traders, it is a great advantage to have an intermediary company that can answer questions even when the markets are closed. You also want a company that allows you to use a variety of trading strategies (not just "buy-and-hold", but day trading or other short-term trading strategies), has easy-to-read charts and offers timely fills (if you buy or sell a stock, the order is executed quickly).

Most online brokerage firms have real-time streaming quotes, easy-to-navigate and secure websites, and clear profit and loss screens. Most likely, they will also have competitive commission rates. In addition, the leading online brokerage firms have educational resources such as webinars and articles on trade and investment.

They may also offer you integrated trading strategies, the ability to customize charts, set up trade alerts, trade options and perhaps trade in overseas markets. These benefits are usually included in the commissions you pay for trading.

I strongly recommend spending time with paper trading before you risk real money. Many brokerage firms have paper trading accounts that allow you to practice trading before you invest real money in the market. There are also websites that allow you to set up and practice trading without real money. To quickly find a reputable online brokerage firm, conduct an Internet search (suggested search terms: "ranking of online brokerage firms", followed by the current year). A list of articles from independent sources will appear. Finally, you can always ask other dealers which brokers they recommend.

Novice traders should seriously consider signing up with one of the leading online brokerage firms. Why? Because of their excellent reputation, online and phone support, and timely order fulfillment. After you gain experience, you may consider the no-frills direct access brokers who offer discounts on commissions for high volume traders.

In addition to competitive rates, the main advantages of direct access are the customizable charts, message and scan data and very fast fills. Advantages like "Fast Fills" are included in the commissions you pay for trading; for others, like messages and data, you sometimes have to pay an additional fee. If you use a broker with direct access, you can also manually select an Electronic Communication Network (EKN), a computerized system that allows traders to trade directly with each other.

Some dealers like to forward their orders directly to an EKN, especially in fast markets. Some online brokerage firms allow you to do this as well. The main advantage of using an EKN is speed. Lack of customer service is the main disadvantage for some brokers with direct access.

Unlike many brokerage firms that patiently discuss all aspects of trading with you, some brokers with direct access only offer help with their software. The good news? These companies compete fiercely for new clients, so many of them offer more services. So talk to them to find out exactly what they offer, how much it will cost and how much support you will receive.

In order to find the best rated placement companies, perform an Internet search (suggested search terms: "listing of the most direct placement companies", followed by the current year).

Questions

Before you register with a brokerage firm, ask many questions or take a close look at their website.

Find out about the monthly fees, commissions and margin rates (the amount of interest you have to pay when you borrow money from the brokerage firm), the type of "chart software" they offer, and whether support is open at night and on weekends.

If possible, experiment with the trading software and charts before opening an account. Some companies will grant you access before you log in. Brokerage companies place great value on active traders like you, so they will try to meet your needs.

Where do I register?

Now that you have chosen a brokerage firm, it is time to open a trading account. Before you are allowed to trade, you must fill out a questionnaire about your trading experience and risk tolerance.

Don't worry about your answers; it is not a test and it will not be used for anything. (In fact, after you make your first trade, the questionnaire is filed away and most likely never looked at again). You will also learn the minimum requirements for opening an account, which can be as much as €2,500, although this will vary from brokerage firm to brokerage firm. You will then be asked whether you would like to open a margin account or a cash account.

Margin simply means that you can borrow money from the brokerage firm when you need it. To give yourself more flexibility, you will probably opt for margin, but just because you can use it does not mean you should. As a beginner, it is best to avoid margin (for now), but it is helpful to have it available. Nevertheless, it is recommended that you learn to trade with your own money before you trade with borrowed money. You do not need to provide a credit report to be eligible for margin; your security is the stocks you buy.

You will also be asked to specify the type of trading style you could use, including day trading. In addition to day trading, you can choose to be an investor or a trader. An investor is a person who buys and holds stocks or other financial instruments for a long period of time; a trader, on the other hand, buys and sells stocks or other financial instruments in the hope of profiting from the short-term price (finally, consider accounts: one for short-term trading and another for long-term investments).

Finally, the brokerage firm will ask you how many deals you intend to make per week or month. However, as soon as you mention day trading, you will have to follow specific rules to ensure that you have the financial resources to maintain a day trading account.

Saving of commissions

The transition to low commissions brought about a revolutionary change in the brokerage industry. In the past, brokers often charged commissions of €100 or more per trade. This forced many people to buy and hold stocks.

When online trading was introduced, expensive commissions became a historical footnote. Today, commissions are typically flat fees of €10 per trade or less, although they vary from company to company. You may also be able to negotiate a "per share" commission. It depends on your trading style and the rates charged by your broker.

For the time being, stick with the payment of a flat fee, and as you gain experience, you can always explore other commission structures. Over time, if you trade a lot, you can negotiate favorable commissions with the brokerage firm. For example, a professional trader would probably pay €0.015 or €0.01 per share. To be profitable, you need to make more money from trading than you pay in commissions.

What is a sample day trader?

Due to past abuses, the National Securities and Exchange Commission has established specific guidelines for all persons who conduct day-to-day business.

If you make more than four daily trades within five business days, you are called a Sample Day Trader. For example, if you buy Coca Cola on Monday and sell the stock before the end of the day, this is called a daytrade.

If you buy Coca Cola on Tuesday and sell it on Wednesday, this is not considered day trade. If you then buy and sell Coca Cola three times on Thursday, this means three more day trades, and you have just reached your quota for the four-day trade. In this example, you will now be referred to as a Sample Day Trader on Thursday.

The full-time day trader

Earning consistently enough money to support yourself and a family can be a challenge for a full-time trader, even with a 50,000 Euro account.

Therefore it is important for you to start with a practice account. If you are consistently successful with it, you may consider trading for a living. But even if you don't make day trading a full-time career, you can use some of these strategies when market conditions are right, or even on a part-time basis.

The Part-Time Day-Trader

If you fear that you won't be able to reach the minimum amount of €25,000 required to be a sample day trader, you have other options. Firstly, you can plan to be a part-time day trader and make no more than four day trades within five business days.

If you choose this strategy, you must carefully monitor your account at all times to ensure that you do not make more than four trades during this five-day period. The main advantage of a part-time day trader is that you can occasionally use day trading strategies without having to meet the strict financial requirements, such as the minimum amount of €25,000.

The disadvantage is that it is not easy to stay within the four trade rule. If the market conditions are right and you see good day trade configurations, you might be tempted to add one or two more trades, but you can't. If you do not have this 25,000 Euro account, you cannot become a sample day trader. It may be a challenge to limit yourself to less than four day trades within five business days, but the alternative is a severe penalty (as mentioned above, your account could be frozen for ninety days). By the time you make your fourth trade, it's too late: you are a sample day trader.

The Sample Day Trader Rule contains other nuances, so it is best to discuss the requirements with the brokerage firm's representatives. However, many of the rules are likely to change over time, so keep up to date by talking to the representatives.

Remember that day trading is not suitable for your retirement planning. Keep this money separate. Use money that you can afford to lose.

Money: Feeling the pain

If it looks like you need a lot of money to make money, remember what the professional trader and market artist William Eckhardt said

"I know a few multimillionaires who started trading with inherited wealth.

In any case, they have lost everything because they did not feel the pain when they lost. In these formative early years of trading, they felt they could afford to lose. They are much better off going to the market with little money and feeling that they cannot afford to lose. I would rather bet on someone who starts with a few thousand euros than someone who starts with millions.

Understanding Margin

If you have a margin account with a broker, you can borrow money from the brokerage company to fund all or part of a trade.

If you do so, there is a margin requirement, i.e. you must have deposited a certain amount of equity (e.g. cash or securities) with the brokerage firm as collateral. How much equity you need depends on a number of factors. If you are an investor or trader (not a daytrader), the brokerage firm will usually lend you up to 50 percent (depending on the stock you buy) of the account value.

This is called margin buying power. When you use Margin, you use leverage, which means that you trade with borrowed money. When you use leverage (i.e. Margin), you can increase potential profits, but you can also increase potential losses. For example, if you had €10,000 and wanted to buy shares, the brokerage firm would probably lend you up to €10,000 extra to buy more shares.

That is a total of 20,000 € (2:1 purchasing power). The exact amount of purchasing power depends on a number of factors, including the type of security you wish to purchase and your margined assets (e.g. some assets, such as bonds, are not margined and cannot be used as equity or collateral). Call your brokerage firm for the exact rules.

Also ask about the interest rate they charge for the margin. It is more than likely that the interest rate will be quite favorable. Sample day traders play by a different, more aggressive set of rules.

Once you are designated as a day trader, you will probably be allowed an intraday leverage of 4:1. For example, if you have €30,000 in your account, you will be given enough buying power to buy securities worth €120,000 (4 × €30,000) in total. This means the total amount for the day and not the amount you can own at any given time.

In other words, you can buy €120,000 worth of securities on Monday, but you cannot hold them overnight. Overnight, the margin requirement is still 2:1, which means that if you use all your intraday buying power (4:1 leverage), you must sell securities before the end of the day to meet the margin requirements (2:1).

If you do not follow these rules, you will receive the dreaded margin call. **In fact, the last call you ever want to receive is a margin call**, which means that you must deposit enough money into your account to meet the margin requirement within twenty-four hours (some brokerage firms give less or sometimes more time, so be sure to ask), or further action may be taken. For example, they may sell your securities immediately to ensure that the margin call is met.

Why margin is so difficult to manage

Most people, especially beginners, find it difficult to manage their margin. In a way, it's like getting an equity loan or credit card with a 30,000 Euro down payment and an additional 90,000 Euro as a loan - very tempting to spend it on a big screen TV instead of the new roof you need.

For many people the use of margin can be an emotional experience because it is so easy to win big or lose big. If you are a newbie, I would recommend not bet on margin until you have gained more knowledge and experience. If a trade works in your favor, margin can definitely accelerate profits. On the other hand, if a trade does not work in your favor, losses can accelerate significantly and it is possible to damage your account.

In the past, many uninformed traders used the margin to bet huge sums of money on ultimately worthless companies like Pets.com and Kozmo.com. When these companies went bankrupt, some dealers went bankrupt as well. **It is painful enough to lose money on the stock market, but losing borrowed money is even worse.** In the end you have to pay back the borrowed money.

If you handle the margin correctly and do not use it as an ATM, it can give you extra leverage. **However, as an inexperienced trader, you should only buy what you can afford and learn to trade with your own money.**

Setting up a home office

Now that you have learned how to open and fund a trading account, the next step is to set up your home office.

While it may be tempting, you don't have to run out and buy a new computer and six monitors. Start slowly and don't invest large sums of money when you set up your day trading business. Most traders set up their office in a remote area of the house so that they can concentrate on making serious financial decisions.

Install a TV with a mute button (so you can watch but not be distracted by financial networks). Keep it simple at first, and you can always add to it as needed and as technology improves.

Buying a desktop computer

Since your computer can make or break you as a daytrader, it is your most important purchase.

You need enough speed and power to run multiple programs, screens and news pages. Day traders need to multitask, so you need high-speed Internet connections and plenty of memory. **No matter what type of computer you use, make sure it is reliable and fast.**

Most brokerage firms work best with Windows-based operating systems, but they strive to meet the needs of Apple users. Check with your brokerage firm for details on the progress they have made. As desktop computers become faster and cheaper, large hard drives, graphics cards, multiple ports and wireless routers are usually standard equipment.

You also need to **invest** in a **reliable backup system in case your hard drive fails.** You need a **high resolution monitor, which should be at least 19 inches (21 inches is better).** Here you will store your charts, order entry screens, streaming quotes and technical indicators. The price of monitors has also gone down, but you should still get a good deal.

Next, you need a **reliable connection to the Internet.** Nowadays, you can connect to your brokerage firm with a DSL or cable modem. Fortunately for consumers, prices are much lower than in recent years, and speeds are improving as competition between Internet providers increases.

Their goal is to trade effectively from home under all market conditions - especially in volatile, fast markets, the kind of environment most day traders crave. It's a personal decision whether to use DSL, cable or even newer technology; all you need is a reliable, fast connection.

Nothing is more frustrating than having to struggle with a slow connection in a fast market. Even worse is that you don't want to go offline in the middle of a trade. You may have to experiment with different setups before making the final decision. Some traders pay a little extra to subscribe to trading newspapers, news sites, or customized or pre-built scanning software that helps them choose which stocks to buy or sell.

First, your brokerage firm should meet the majority of your immediate trading needs. As your experience grows, you may also pay for additional features (news feeds and scanning software). Again, you should start slowly and only buy what you really need.

Trading from a laptop

Most professional traders use desktop computers and may use a laptop in emergencies or on vacation.

Nevertheless, the latest generation of laptop computers is quite remarkable. The advantage of laptops is of course the freedom to trade anywhere in the world. In the past, most laptops had extremely small screens, but now some of the biggest laptops have plenty of room for your news pages, order entry and charts.

With a few mouse or touchpad clicks you can see a lot of data. The professionals who work from a laptop tend to connect a second 19- or 21-inch monitor to keep track of all the information.

It is possible to trade from a laptop, but you may need to buy a second or maybe a third high resolution monitor. Brokerage firms enable their clients to trade on the go with a variety of mobile devices, including cell phones and tablets. Whether you can consistently make money with these devices is debatable (you may need to see more charts and information than they can display), but they are ideal for emergencies. Undoubtedly, there are still devices that have yet to be invented to make trading on the go even easier.

Protect your computer

Use a top-of-the-line surge protector to protect your equipment. An accidental lightning strike could leave you with a fried computer.

Install the latest anti-virus software and - just as important - Internet security software. It's amazing how many people make financial transactions worth thousands of dollars on unsecured computers with outdated virus software. Hackers are constantly attacking vulnerable computers and looking for potential vulnerabilities.

Most brokerage firms spend millions of dollars to protect their online computer accounts from attacks, but for much less money you can also protect your home computer. This includes keeping up to date with computer corrections and system updates, especially if you have a Windows-based system, as they are more vulnerable to viruses. Make sure you have both a physical firewall, most likely built into your router, and a software firewall that comes with your Windows software.

When you set up a wireless network in your home, you immediately create a secure password so that your neighbors or passers-by cannot piggyback on your Internet connection. Each password should contain a combination of letters and numbers. If you use your laptop outside your home, be careful when using public hotspots for stock trading. Clever hackers may be able to view information you send from your computer to a wireless access point. If you routinely trade at a remote location, you can buy a broadband card from one of the major wireless carriers that offers the most secure connection.

If not, stay online as long as possible. **Most importantly, never use public computers or kiosks for financial transactions**; this could compromise all your account information, including passwords. Many computers, whether public or not, are equipped with keystroke logging software that records each of your transactions, including password collection. If you do not follow these basic rules, your account could be at risk when you return to your hotel or home.

What kind of trading strategy do you use?

Now that you have a better idea of how to choose a brokerage firm and set up your home office, let's learn more about trading strategies.

There is no single strategy for retailers that fits everyone. The strategies depend on your personality and trading style. A strategy that works well for one trader may not make sense for another trader. Besides day trading, you may want to try other trading strategies that have worked well in the past.

Of course, past performance is no guarantee of future results. However, there may be times when you want to give up day trading in favor of a more lucrative approach.

Here are three of the most recognized trading strategies:

SWING TRADING

Unlike day traders, who rarely hold or hold positions overnight, swing traders attempt to make stock gains over a short period of time, typically two to five days.

Although they are not tied to a specific time frame, swing traders usually buy at the beginning of the week, but are available again in cash on weekends. Many professional traders use more than one trading style. Therefore, under certain market conditions, they can switch from day trading to swing trading. Swing trading, especially during short-term trend markets, may be the right strategy.

POSITION TRADING

Unlike day traders or swing traders, position traders hold positions for longer periods of time, usually several weeks or months, but possibly longer. However, unlike buy-and-hold investors, position traders will not hold a position indefinitely and sell a position when profits are realized (or to limit losses).

In many ways, position trading is similar to swing trading, but with a longer holding period.

SCALPING

Before decimalization, scalping was all the rage. In those days, traders tried to quickly get 0.25 euros or more per share within seconds or minutes, trade thousands of shares and quickly charge 200 to 500 euros per trade.

It was much more difficult than it seemed. At the time, a few popular books written about scalping were misleading - they made scalping sound like a simple strategy that anyone can do, when in reality it is very, very difficult for most people. The practice probably cost people a lot of money. As a day trader, you will probably scalp from time to time, i.e. enter and exit a stock within seconds or minutes to make a quick profit. The idea is to make many trades (from five to hundreds) but aim for smaller profits. Keep in mind, however, that this is a stressful trading method that can result in losses due to commissions.

CHAPTER 2: Reading Charts

To be a daytrader, you need a set of powerful tools that allow you to determine when to enter and exit the market.

The most common tool is the stock chart. When you view a stock chart, you are looking at the history: you see how stock prices move up or down over time. The chart can help you find statistical clues that can give you an advantage over other traders. Using a stock chart means that you do not rely solely on your emotions when making trading decisions.

Traders say that a picture is worth a thousand words, and you will see why when you analyze charts. By studying them, you can determine whether buyers or sellers dominate the market, which can help you find stocks that are on the move, the kind of stocks that can turn into profitable businesses. Stock charts are based on a universal language, technical analysis, a method of valuing securities based on price movements and volumes.

Nearly everyone can understand this language after some studies. Technical analysis helps you make statistical assumptions about a stock, which can increase your chances of successful trading. When you look at a stock chart, you are looking primarily at the price and volume. An alternative method of analyzing stocks is fundamental analysis or the study of the underlying data that affects a company. For example, fundamental analysts look at profits, assets and liabilities, competitive companies and the actions of corporate insiders. Some traders use a combination of fundamental and technical analysis, using fundamental analysis to find good companies and technical analysis to determine when to enter or exit.

As a day trader you will almost always use technical analysis. When you call up a stock chart on a screen, you can choose between different time frames ranging from minutes, hours, days or months. Day traders will use very short time frames: 5-minute, 15-minute, 30-minute and 60-minute charts. Sometimes they will show a daily chart for longer term trades and maybe a weekly chart to identify a longer term trend.

Chart Basics

Charts are displayed on your computer screen when you log into your broker account. They are constantly updated and have many features, all of which can be customized. Let's take a look at some of the terms you will read and hear over and over again during the technical analysis.

Understanding support and resistance

Support and resistance are key words in technical analysis, and it is important that you understand how they work.

When the stock price moves up or down on a chart, it can basically slow down or accelerate suddenly when it reaches support or resistance levels. Understanding support and resistance helps you know when to enter or exit a position (a stock or other security).

The concept of support and resistance is actually quite simple: if a stock touches support, which is similar to a floor, it may be a good time to buy (because the price is likely to rise). And if a stock encounters resistance that is similar to a floor, it may be a good time to sell (because the price is likely to go down). Consider support and resistance as one trading zone, not as exact price levels.

To be even more precise: Support is the price at which the price of a stock has stopped falling and has either moved sideways (e.g. the price moves in a horizontal pattern) or in the opposite direction. At this level, selling pressure has eased and demand for the stock has been strong enough to prevent a further decline in price. The demand will exceed the supply and prevent the price from falling further.

Resistance, on the other hand, is the price at which selling pressure is strong enough to prevent the share from rising further. Supply exceeds demand and the pressure to buy has ceased. More sellers will enter the market and prevent the share from rising further.

Technicians analyze charts to determine what happens to a stock when it reaches important support or resistance levels. Often the price of a stock reverses and bounces off a support or resistance level.

Many day traders take action when a stock breaks through the support or resistance level. When you look at a chart, you always want to identify these levels. The key point is to determine how the stock or market will react when it approaches the support or resistance level. Will it break through or will it reverse? To answer this important question, you will probably spend hours studying charts. It is not a skill that can be learned quickly.

Important Note: When a resistance is broken, this level often turns into support. Conversely, when the support is broken through, it often becomes the new resistance level.

Volume rules

In conjunction with price, volume has always been one of the most important indicators to watch.

The volume is simply the number of shares traded in a given period. The volume is usually displayed at the bottom of a chart. Technicians who study volume observe an incredible amount of information.

For example, you look to see whether a share or market has a higher or lower daily volume than in previous days. In what way is this useful? When you combine volume with price, you get extremely important information about whether the stock (or market) will continue to rise or fall, or whether the direction could be reversed. As with anything that has to do with the stock market, you need to take your time to study these clues. Basically, the volume is tabulated by a computer that collects all tick data (price movements) and draws the volume bars.

As the volume increases and the dynamic increases, the volume bars increase. Conversely, if the volume decreases and the dynamics decreases, the volume bars decrease.

To confirm an optimistic outbreak, the technicians want to see if a stock is moving up at higher volumes and if the movement is accompanied by broad-based buying activity. This is a positive sign for the bulls. On the other hand, a stock that falls at higher volumes could signal the beginning of a short-term correction. It is an indication that new buyers are reluctant to jump in to buy. What makes a stock go up or down? Buyers push the stock up and sellers push the stock down. However, one problem with examining the volume is that you do not know who is responsible for the increased volume: buyers or sellers.

Therefore, it is important to use volume to confirm what you see on the chart and not to trade based on volume data alone. In addition, the increased popularity of high frequency trading has distorted some of the volume statistics. For example, it may look like a stock is attracting buying interest, but that only comes from high-speed computers that scalp for pennies.

It is similar to a car that is in neutral and turns its engine: it makes a lot of noise, but it doesn't go anywhere. Again, it is important that you investigate the volume in conjunction with the price. Note: You will also hear people talking about liquidity, i.e. how easy it is for traders to get in or out of a stock at a single price. Liquid shares are filled quickly and you can buy or sell them immediately. Illiquid stocks are much more difficult to sell at a competitive price. As you can imagine, day traders need liquid shares to get in and out quickly.

Recognizing the trend

The whole purpose of viewing a chart is to determine in which direction the stock is moving: up, down or sideways.

Charts help traders to recognize the trend. By recognizing the trend, traders decide whether to follow the trend, wait for it to retreat (when the stock price drops from its peak) or simply stay on the sidelines. A glance at a chart can help determine which direction the stock is currently moving in. The challenge, of course, is to find out when the trend might end.

Let us take a look at the three types of trends: Upward trend, downward trend and sideways trend.

TRADE AN UPWARD TREND

The popular "follow-the-trend" strategy has been very successful for retailers over the years. You may even have heard the saying: "The trend is your friend".

Nothing is sweeter than buying at the beginning of a trend and following it to its end. If a stock climbs higher and higher, it is in an upward trend. For many traders the easiest and most profitable strategy is to follow an uptrend. Sometimes stocks rise so fast that they "break out" above the current resistance level and move dramatically upwards.

It is very profitable for traders to own a stock that breaks out. To be precise, an uptrend occurs when the stock price makes a series of higher highs and higher lows that you can see on a chart. For example, if you look at the price pattern on a chart, a higher high is when today's intraday high (the stock price) is higher than yesterday's intraday high. A higher low is when today's intraday low is higher than yesterday's intraday low.

Several higher highs and higher lows form an uptrend. Unfortunately, not all markets or stocks work together. Although the ideal environment for almost all traders and investors is an uptrend, many markets are restless and volatile. However, day traders can find an uptrend on any chart, from the minute to the daily chart. As a day trader, you will primarily use intraday charts such as the 60-minute, 15-minute and 5-minute charts to make entries and exits.

SURVIVE A DOWNWARD TREND

The opposite of an uptrend is a downtrend, when a stock moves deeper and deeper and deeper. Sometimes stocks move so low that they collapse below the current support level and move down dramatically.

It is a situation where you lose money if you are in a downtrend for a long time (you bought the stock assuming the price would go up). To be more precise, a downtrend occurs when the stock price makes a series of lower highs and lows. You can see them in the graph. For example, if you look at the price pattern when today's intraday low (the stock price) is lower than yesterday's intraday low, it is a lower low.

A lower high is when today's intraday high is lower than yesterday's intraday high. Several lower lows and lower highs result in a downward trend. Long, agonizingly slow downtrends, which I call death by a thousand cuts, can be frustrating for investors and traders. Suddenly, in the middle of a downtrend, the market can have a fast, fear-induced selling frenzy that takes everyone by surprise. As a result, stock prices will collapse.

SIDEWAYS PATTERN

No share rises forever, so that the share is eventually exhausted when the sellers overtake the buyers. At this point the share moves sideways or even falls in price.

You may see a pattern that, according to technical analysts, is simply behavior displayed on a screen. With experience, you will be able to spot patterns immediately and perhaps get clues as to what the market or an individual stock might do.

The sideways pattern can be very frustrating for traders as the stock goes up and down without even going anywhere. The sideways trend can last for days or weeks, but if you study the trends closely, you will learn that there are three types of sideways or horizontal patterns: Trading in a range, congestion and consolidation. Let's start with a closer look at the three types of sideways patterns.

SPAN WIDTH

A share in a trading range can be quite frustrating for some people. A margin is the difference between the highest and lowest price of a stock. In other words, a spread means that a stock moves up and down in a horizontal range between support and resistance.

In fact, investors or long-term traders seem unable to make a profit if a stock reaches the upper or lower edge of a range and reverses direction. In the short term, the stock moves, but does not break out of the trading range. It continues to move between support and resistance.

If you as a day trader can recognize these reversals, you can live a decent life as a trader - but nobody said it was easy! Buying when a stock falls and selling when it rallies is a challenging strategy, but it's a skill you need to develop if you're serious as a trader. This is the heart and soul of day trading. It also takes a lot of practice to buy when a stock is falling and sell when it is fluctuating between support and resistance on an intraday chart. Also, the trading range on an intraday chart is usually much narrower than on a daily or weekly chart.

OVERLOAD

If a stock is trading in a range, you can make money if you choose the right time. But if a stock is in a bottleneck pattern, it is not going anywhere.

The author and dealer Toni Turner jokingly says that she has a blocked nose. In a traffic jam the stock fluctuates in a tight, unpredictable pattern that makes trading extremely difficult. In addition, the volume during the pattern is low. Turner gives the following advice: "If you notice a stock jam, stay away.

Do not kiss your friends who have a cold and do not trade stocks that are traded in congestion patterns unless you want your trading account to get sick. Most traders avoid stocks that are in a congestion pattern, although in this example the stock suddenly broke out of the trading range and moved higher.

CONSOLIDATION

The third sideways pattern is consolidation, which often appears in charts as a very compressed, fluctuating line. Consolidation reflects the struggle between buyers and sellers, and when this stock pattern finally ends, it could violently move in both directions, up or down.

This is the reason why so many dealers like to deviate from this pattern. If you can determine in which direction the stock will move, then this pattern will be profitable. The challenge, however, is to make an accurate prediction. (Hopefully, turning a pattern into a profitable trade will be one of your goals).

Note: Although it is difficult to predict whether a stock will fall above or below a consolidation pattern, there are often indications. For example, look for an increasing volume, which indicates that the stock could make a sudden move. Also, in an uptrend, the stock has a better chance of rising higher out of this pattern. On the other hand, in a downtrend the stock could suddenly fall. The longer a stock trades in a consolidation pattern, the more explosive the potential movement becomes when it breaks above the resistance levels or below the support levels.

Understanding time periods

As mentioned earlier, day traders use short-term time frames, such as 5-minute, 15-minute, 30-minute, 60-minute charts and a daily chart for a longer-term view.

You can also choose weekly or monthly charts to get an even bigger picture. This is a reality check that helps you to identify the primary trend. Many traders do not want to bet on rising prices when the daily trend is down. The time frame you use for day trading is a personal decision.

Experiment until you find your own preferred time frame. For example, Toni Turner likes to use an 8-minute chart, while other traders often use a 5-minute or 10-minute chart. "I like to use 8-minute charts for day trading," says Turner, "instead of the 5-minute charts that most traders use.

I like to get off the fives" because most other traders use 5, 10 or 15 minute charts. I also use 13-minute charts. I use daily charts to determine the primary trend, support and resistance and the entry price. Then I drift down to my intraday charts to execute entries". No matter what time frame you choose, whether 10-minute, 60-minute or daily charts, always look at the stock over a period of several days. If you look at a 10-minute chart, you are looking at it over a period of two to three days. You want to see if the stock rises above the previous day's high or if it is weak compared to yesterday. A month is probably too long if you are day trading, a few days are recommended.

Chart types

Now that you have a basic understanding of chart vocabulary, we will take a closer look at the three most popular chart types. When you expand a chart, you choose which type you want to display: Line, Bar or Candle. Each of these types has advantages and disadvantages, which we will discuss.

Chart lines

In the past, many Western traders relied on two-dimensional line charts to provide a visual snapshot of the stock market. A line chart simply represents the closing price of a stock over a period of time. Then a line connects each price point. They are the easiest to use and visually appealing, especially when viewed on television, in PowerPoint presentations or in books.

Although long-term investors or traders sometimes use line charts for a "big picture" view of the market, line charts do not provide much detailed information. **Conclusion: day traders usually need more information than a line chart can provide.**

More details: Bar charts

A bar chart provides more details about market opening, closing, high and low. A bar chart includes a horizontal scale at the bottom of the chart with a price range for almost any time period.

The "bar" is the price range of the share for the period. For example, in a daily chart, the upper part of the bar represents the highest sold price for the day, while the lower part of the bar represents the lowest price for the day. Each bar also has a short horizontal line extending to the left and right.

The left line represents the opening price for the trading day and the right line marks the closing price. By examining a bar chart in combination with the volume, smart traders can get an indication of who controls the market: buyer or seller. Bottom line: Bar charts are more useful than line charts, but day traders probably want to use the next chart type: Candle. This can really help you to read the thoughts of the market.

See who is in control: Candle Diagrams

Day traders need even more information than line or bar charts, which is why candlestick charts are so popular.

They show the spread between the opening and closing price of a share during a given period. With a glance at a candle, experienced traders can immediately see if the bulls or bears are in control and if a reversal is possible.

When combined with traditional technical indicators (formulas displayed in a chart to determine the future price movements of a stock or other security), candlestick charts can be a powerful source of information. With a little experience, candle charts are also relatively easy to interpret.

Toni Turner put it this way: "Candles are a powerful source of information: "Candles charts are the luxury version of bar charts. It's like switching from a black and white TV to a living color TV.

Conclusion: It is recommended to use candlestick charts, because they provide a large amount of information and visual clues.

THE HISTORY OF THE CANDLE DIAGRAMS

Candles are actually the oldest form of technical analysis, originally created by Munehisa Homma, a wealthy Japanese rice merchant, in the eighteenth century.

Steve Nison, president of Candlecharts.com and author of the best-selling Japanese Candlestick Charting Techniques (Prentice-Martinl, 2001), was the first to introduce candles to the West. "The Japanese say that every candle tells a story," says Nison. "The candle has the same information as the bar chart, but it is constructed differently. By using candles, you can visually see who is in control of the market at the time the candle is made".

CANDLE BODY

The candle has two main components, the real body and shadow.

The real body is the rectangular part of the candlestick and shows the range between the opening price of the stock and its closing price. With a quick look at the real body you can get clues as to whether the bulls or bears dominate the market.

The study of the color of the real body gives important information. If the real body is white (or clear), it simply means that the closing price was higher than the opening price, a bullish sign. The larger and longer the white real body is, the more bullish it is. During an auction you want to see a row of long white candles, preferably at a higher volume. On the other hand, a black (or filled) real body means that the closing body was lower than the opening price. The higher and longer the black real body is, the bearer it is. A row of long black candles may indicate that the bears are now in control. "We get nervous as the real body gets smaller and smaller because it means that supply and demand are becoming more equal," Nison explains. In other words, long white candles reflect strong buying pressure, while long black candles reflect strong selling pressure. Short candles reflect that prices are consolidating, i.e. not moving too far in one direction or the other.

SHADOWS

The shadows of a candle are the thin lines that protrude above or below the real body. The shadows reflect the ups or downs of the day.

The shadow above the real body is the upper shadow, while the shadow below the real body is the lower shadow. For example, a long upper shadow indicates that the day's high was far above the open and close.

Conversely, a long lower shadow indicates that the day's low was far below the open and close. It gives traders an indication of whether the buyer or seller is in control. Therefore, a candle with a long upper shadow and a short lower shadow indicates that buyers are in control; prices rose. Conversely, a candlestick with a long lower shadow and a short upper shadow indicates that the sellers are in control, so prices went down.

Open and Close

The more experience you gain, the clearer it becomes that the most important part of each day is opening and closing. Traders are often quite emotional when they place their orders at the opening. Even the last hour is volatile as many traders close their positions.

As a control: The top of the candle body represents the closing price, while the bottom represents the opening price. If the candle body is hollow or white, the closing price was higher than the opening price. If the candle body is black, the closing price was lower than the opening price. At a glance you can discover detailed information about the security.

Drawing trend lines

Have you ever played the Connect the Dots game? It's the same with drawing trend lines.

(However, instead of points, you connect a series of highs and lows on a chart to confirm a trend). Drawing trend lines helps you determine support and resistance. This can help you determine when to enter or exit a stock. You can use your brokerage firm's software to draw trend lines or, if you want to do it the old-fashioned way, take out a ruler and connect the highs and lows.

By drawing two trend lines, one connecting the highs and one connecting the lows, you create what analysts call a channel (or envelope). Creating a channel can help you determine price targets (a projected price) based on the concepts of support and resistance. By drawing trend lines, you can see in a chart when a stock or index reaches higher highs and higher lows (uptrends). Conversely, you can also see if a stock reaches lower lows and lower highs (downtrend). In both examples, an increase in volume reinforces the upward and downward trends. You can look at the volume bars to see if the volume supports the up or down movement.

CHAPTER 3: Interpreting Patterns

You can look at the chart patterns to find stocks you want to buy or sell, although for you as a daytrader newbie these patterns may be one of the last instruments you need to study.

It takes practice to interpret them correctly. Some inexperienced traders make a few trades based on patterns, only to watch them fail and give up. For this reason, you don't want to trade based on just one pattern.

Instead, use technical indicators to confirm what you think you are seeing. Some traders see the patterns immediately, while others look but don't notice anything. If you are indeed good at pattern recognition, you will want to explore the dozens of other patterns you will see in the charts. I have included a list of additional sources in the "Resources" appendix if you want to learn more. If patterns are not your strongest area, remember only the most important ones (like those included in this chapter). Fortunately, the more you study diagrams, the better you will be able to recognize patterns. If you keep a trading diary to record your trading experiences (a practice I highly recommend), be sure to keep track of the patterns that work for you and those that don't. Let's start by taking a look at the key patterns that are most useful for day traders. Many of these chart patterns are used in very short periods of time, such as a 5-minute, 30-minute or 60-minute chart.

Basic Chart Patterns

These chart patterns are the most popular ones used by day traders. As mentioned earlier, it can be difficult to trade based on patterns, and as a newbie, this will not be your first priority. Apart from that, it is useful to learn the most basic patterns if you see them on a chart.

Double bottom (BULLICAL)

A common pattern for a bullish reversal is the double bottom, which looks like a "W". After an extended downtrend, the stock has failed to break through the support after two attempts and is recovering higher.

After the pattern is completed, the trend changes from "bearish to bullish". However, there is always the chance that the stock will consolidate or stagnate before breaking through resistance and moving up. Before the first breakout, look for an early increase in volume on the lower left side. Although this is an easily recognizable pattern, the double bottom does not always give a viable signal. Therefore, be sure to confirm this with other technical indicators before making a trade based on this pattern.

Double tip (BÄRIG)

The double peak, which looks like an "M", is a significant retrograde reversal pattern that shows two peaks at the same price level. After an upward trend, the stock failed to break through the resistance after two attempts.

After the pattern is completed, the trend changes from bullish to bearish. There is always a chance that the stock will move sideways before breaking through the support and moving much lower. Look for an increase in volume near the upper left corner before the stock goes down. Just like the double bottom, the double top is easy to spot, but does not always give a usable signal. As always, you will want to confirm with technical indicators before trading based on this pattern.

Head and shoulders (Bearded)

The reversal pattern of head and shoulders is very evident in the charts, indicating that purchases have been stopped at the top of the trend and have the potential to reverse direction.

The stock moves up and then retracts to form the left shoulder. It then moves higher to form the head, but cannot break through the support and forms the neckline.

Finally, the shaft rises again to form the right shoulder, but it does not succeed in breaking through the resistance. At this point, this pattern shows us that the shaft is doomed when it falls below the neckline. Besides observing the course, you will also examine the volume. In general, the head is formed on reduced volume, which indicates that the buying pressure is not as strong as when you first climb on the left shoulder. The volume should decrease on the right shoulder for the pattern to take effect. On the last attempt on the right shoulder, the volume should be even less than the head, indicating that the buying volume has disappeared. An inverted head and shoulders that is bullish is the exact opposite of the head and shoulders.

GAPS (hereinafter also gaps)

A gap occurs when a share is opened at a different price than the price on the previous day when it was closed. For example, if Microsoft closed at €23.80 on Wednesday and then opened at €24.55 on Thursday, there would be a gap of €0.75 in the chart. Gaps that appear as open areas in a chart where no trading has taken place are the result of an imbalance between buy and sell orders.

Gaps are caused by current news or profit reports or because there is no trading at a certain price level.

When this happens, the stock suddenly jumps, reflecting strong buying or selling pressure in the stock. Gaps occur most often in a daily chart, but you can also see them in intraday trading.

An intraday gap almost always occurs with stocks that are only traded a little. An intraday gap does not often occur with a normal share that has a decent volume (exception: a midday news item). Most gaps occur before or after trading. Sometimes traders are heard to talk about "filling the gap", which simply means that the price will go down or go back to the last price before the gap, which will cause the gap to close. In the example above, Microsoft would fill the gap by tracing back up to €23.80

There are actually four types of gaps:

Standard Gaps

These uneventful gaps occur relatively frequently, perhaps caused by an imbalance in order.

It is more than likely that the volume will be relatively small and the gap will be filled or closed relatively quickly. Gaps often occur when a stock moves sideways. A common gap will probably not offer you a trading opportunity, especially if the volume is small. Most technicians advise against trading it at all.

Outbreak Gaps

The gap that breaks out can be most profitable and exciting if you own stocks before it breaks out.

Suddenly the equity gap gapes upwards, perhaps at a higher than normal volume. This could be the beginning of a significant upward movement, the bulls hope. It is possible that if the volume is high, the stock will move further up in the same direction as the gap.

Even if the gap is closed at some point, this may not happen immediately, which is why traders like tearing gaps. In fact, it could take a long time to fill the gap. Some professional traders like to buy breakout gaps right at the opening (not recommended for beginners, as stock prices sometimes fall rapidly at the opening. If you are riding a breakout gap, you may not want to take your profits immediately, especially if you buy the stock overnight. Why? This could be the beginning of a new uptrend. Assuming you have profits at the end of the day, you will probably switch from a day trader to a swing trader. Once again, no one said that trading is easy!

Outlier Gap (also called measurement gap)

Just as with the breakout gap, the breakout gap suddenly gapes upward due to the higher volume and increased buyer enthusiasm.

Sometimes there is a sudden pullback before the stock breaks out and continues to rise. It is as if the stock stops or rests before resuming its previous trend. You may wonder what the difference is between a breakout and a breakout gap. According to the technicians, the "breakout gap" occurs in the middle of a trend, while the "breakout gap" starts a new trend. Don't worry if you find it difficult to distinguish between the different gaps; it definitely takes experience to successfully deal with them. With much more experience, you will eventually learn the nuances of exploiting gaps and perhaps also when to identify profitable opportunities. Simple? No. Possible? Yes.

Exhaustion Gaps

In the end all good gaps come to an end. After the stock has moved higher and higher, the gap suddenly gapes to a higher than normal volume.

Then, late in the trend, after the big price movement, the stock is exhausted and demand falls.

A correction may be imminent. The share will slow down if the share price falters. Since exhaustion gaps are often quickly followed by a reversal, informed traders will immediately enter sell orders as soon as they realize that the gap is ending, which could result in a mad breakout from the stock. In addition, the volume may increase when previous buyers notice the exhaustion and unload their shares. Hopefully you will be out of the stock before it reverses, because now it might feel like it is too late to get out.

Chart patterns for experienced traders

Now that you are familiar with the most basic patterns, it is time to go one step further.

The following patterns are not difficult to recognize, but turning them into a profitable business requires skill and experience. Learning how to recognize these patterns can be useful, but do not worry if you cannot "see" some of them. Just draw trend lines to make them more visible. Most chart programs allow you to draw lines, which makes patterns easier to recognize.

"Triangles"

A common pattern is a triangle that is part of a continuation pattern.

To refresh your memory: A continuation pattern means that the stock simply continues to move in the same direction, perhaps taking a break (consolidation), but the stock trend remains intact. The continuation pattern can be bullish or bearish, but the trend is not interrupted. There are three main types of triangles: ascending, descending and symmetrical triangles. With a little practice you will start to see triangles everywhere!

Ascending triangles

In an ascending triangle, the share price makes higher lows, but the highs remain the same, indicating that resistance is strong in this area.

Nonetheless, each time this price moves away from the resistance level, away from this area, bulls are willing to enter earlier and earlier to buy, creating the rising triangle pattern. A breakout is inevitable when the two lines converge. When the apex of the triangle is formed, the bottom line of the triangle acts as a support, while the top line of the triangle acts as resistance.

Descending triangles

The descending triangle is an inverted image of an ascending triangle. A descending triangle makes a decline a new low.

Each time the stock tries to recover, the bears are willing to enter earlier and earlier and try to sell the stock, creating the pattern of the descending triangle. Where the two lines converge, it is possible that a downward breakout will occur.

When the triangle point is formed, again the bottom line of the triangle acts as support, while the top line of the triangle acts as resistance.

Symmetrical triangles

Small symmetrical triangles are called flags and pennants. Many dealers claim that flags (and pennants) are among the most reliable signals. (Unfortunately, technical analysis is not 100 percent accurate, but some patterns are more reliable than others).

Continuation patterns like flags and pennants let a stock rest by moving sideways for a while before it tends to move further up or down. "It is the pause that refreshes," some traders jokingly say. Remember that a pennant resembles a small triangle, but its trend lines converge as the pattern is formed. Ideally, after the pattern is completed, there is a strong movement up or down and the lines converge, creating the pennant.

Flags

Flags are short-term continuation patterns that reflect a short pause (consolidation) after a rapid movement before it starts again.

You will want to see if the volume increases during the formation of the pattern. Although they resemble a pennant, the trend lines of a flag are almost parallel. When you see this pattern on a chart, it really looks like a flag (and it often has a pole on both sides)! Note: A bear flag looks like an inverted flag on a flagpole.

Candle Pattern

Many retailers look at candle pattern formations to get hints on when to buy or sell. Candle charts are often used to provide clues about market psychology or trend changes.

Here are some of the most popular candlestick patterns:

The Doji

The doji is a very common candle pattern, characterized by small, thin lines and an equal opening and closing price.

The educated cross is the doji, which is often interpreted as the indecision between bears and bulls. If you see a stock forming a doji top, you might consider taking money off the table after confirming with other indicators.

The doji is a clear warning signal. In addition, there are variations of the doji, such as the tombstone doji (opening and closing occur at the lowest point of the day, indicating an important turning point in the direction of the trend) and the doji with long legs (opening and closing are almost the same, indicating indecision).

"The dark cloud cover"

The dark cloud cover is another common candle pattern that is considered quite reliable. It is very useful in identifying market peaks. When it looks like a cloudy day, this pattern often shows that buyers are giving up and sellers are becoming more aggressive.

Hammer

The hammer, a bullish reversal pattern, has a short real body that is at the top of the trading range for the day.

When you see it for the first time, it really looks like a hammer! Often the hammer is formed at the end of a share advance, in this case it is a hanging man. When the hammer forms at the end of a stock drop, it is called a lower-tail hammer.

How to use the candle pattern

One of the most common candle patterns is the bearish intertwining pattern, where the black real body wraps around the white real body.

This has a greater probability of inversion than the dark cloud cover. But it is even more reliable, he says, if a candle pattern confirms a traditional Western pattern.

You can use candle to confirm the pattern and have a higher probability of a trade being made. For example, you could use the dark cloud cover to confirm the resistance, which is a stronger signal than a dark cloud cover itself.

The key is to understand that candles reflect market psychology. Therefore, I suggest that you focus on the patterns that make the most sense for you. You will find many doji patterns in a chart, but because they are so common, they are not so important in an intraday chart. One of the advantages of candlestick charts is that they show the power of the current movement. For example, if you have a hammer at the bottom of a recent downtrend, the candle will indicate that less of that downtrend is losing momentum. What is important for day traders is to examine each candle line for signals. If you have a series of hammers, a series of lower shadows in the same support area, it shows you that either demand is coming or supply is drying up.

Incorrect use of candles

It is not surprising that some retailers misuse candles.

Many people see the doji and believe that there will be a reversal. A doji during an uptrend means that the market has gone from a neutral to a neutral market.

It does not mean that it has gone from an uptrend to a downtrend. It increases the probability of reversal, but it does not make it 100 percent. The key to being an informed trader, he suggests, is candlestick training.

Another example of the misuse of candles is the hammer candle signal. Maybe you have a hammer signal that you should not buy. On the other hand, you might have a hammer signal that could be a great buying opportunity. We call this a candle in context. Look at the candle in the prism of the current market.

For example, he would combine technical concepts such as support and resistance and the general market direction with candle signals. If the hammer is within a longer-term trend, however you define it, and the hammer confirms a support level, and if there is a good risk return to trading, I would be more aggressive in buying than a hammer that is within a longer-term downtrend.

Other abuses of candles are that they are used alone without technical indicators and that one does not pay attention to money management before placing a trade. It is especially important that you use stop loss orders. I place my stops with candle signals, for example below the low of the hammer. I prefer to wait for the market to close, but if you trade intraday and you cannot wait for the market to close, you need to place certain intraday stops. Sometimes it is too late for day traders to wait for the market to close, so you have to place intraday stops. I use the candle to set "stopout levels", for example, the high of the shooting star, the high of the doji or the low of the hammer or the low of the bullish devouring pattern.

It is very important to first determine whether a trade has a favorable risk-return. You might have a great candle signal, but if it is not a good risk-return, the candle does not matter. The biggest problem with candles is that people recognize a pattern and buy immediately. Even if you have a candle signal, you should confirm with Western technicians. The mistake people make is to rely only on candlesticks. They should not be considered in isolation. In fact, one of the limitations of candles is that they do not set price targets. Candlesticks are good at identifying highs and lows and knowing when to get out, but you need Western technical analysis to get price targets. That's why our training focuses on the best candlesticks with the best Western indicators.

CHAPTER 4: Use of technical indicators

As you learn more about day trading, you will increasingly rely on a number of instruments called technical indicators.

These are the crooked little lines that are drawn on, above or below a stock chart. They measure the short-term price activity of a stock in various ways to predict the future price movement of the stock. Usually you select indicators from a drop-down list next to the chart.

They are used to increase the chances for successful trading. Many day traders use technical indicators to make trading decisions. For example, the use of indicators is used to determine when the market or an individual security is overbought or oversold. When too much is bought (overbought) or sold (oversold), this is an indication that there may be a reversal.

Why? Because if a share or an index has risen too strongly and too quickly, there is often a retreat. Identifying overbought and oversold conditions is only one way to use technical indicators. Some traders use technical indicators to try to predict or anticipate the direction of stocks or indices. Although indicators are helpful, don't make the usual mistake of letting them make the buying and selling decisions for you.

Indicators provide important information about market conditions, but in the end you make the trading decision. You have to put all the pieces together to make a diagnosis. Although there are hundreds of technical indicators, many are too slow to be useful for day traders. Therefore I will focus on a number of indicators that are popular with many day traders. In the end you will find a handful of indicators that are useful for you and your trading methodology. If you have never used indicators before, this chapter may seem a bit overwhelming at first. However, after you have used indicators a few times, you will find that they are easy to insert into a chart (but not always easy to interpret).

Find indicators

Although you will soon be familiar with a number of indicators, you do not want to have more than four or five on a chart at once.

Some traders use so many indicators that they are afflicted by a condition called "indicatoritis", as one financial blogger put it. Unfortunately, there is no magic indicator that can give you all the answers.

Indicators simply point you in the right direction by giving you clues as to what may occur. Sometimes the indicators contradict each other, so you have to act as a referee and determine which one conveys the right message. For example, one indicator can generate a buy signal while another indicator generates a sell signal. Often some indicators work well in one market environment but not well in another.

For example, moving averages (MA) work well in a trend environment, but are not as effective in a volatile market. **The indicators you will read about next should not be considered as actionable trades, but only as guidelines.** Always use other indicators as confirmation before buying or selling a stock or index.

The most popular indicator: Moving Average

Moving averages are one of the most popular technical indicators and often the most reliable, regardless of your time frame.

To be precise, moving averages show the value of the price of a security over a period of time, e.g. the last 20, 50, 100 or 200 days. If you superimpose the moving average on the stock price, the relationship between the moving average and the price becomes visible.

Here too, the experienced eye can detect valuable clues as to how the share price might react. Moving averages are easy to understand and, if interpreted correctly, can lead to profitable business. When moving averages are plotted, trends (as mentioned above) can be identified quickly. Most importantly, moving averages often signal when a trend can begin or end. The two most common moving averages are the simple moving average (SMA) and the exponential moving average (EMA).

The Simple Moving Average

Many people use the simple moving average because it is the default in most charting programs. For example, a simple 10-day moving average is calculated by taking the average of the last 10 days of the closing price of the stock and dividing it by 10.

So if the tenth day is added, the first day is omitted. In other words, old days are deleted as soon as new days become available. The moving averages move constantly. As the process is repeated every day, a smooth line is created, which can be displayed in a diagram. The longer the time frame, the stronger the signal, another reason why even day traders need to study multiple time frames.

Why is a 5-day MA more meaningful than a 1-day MA? More data is used in the calculation, therefore it is more time-saving. Furthermore, a 60-minute chart is more meaningful than a 5-minute chart. As a day trader you will use short time frames: minutes and hours. Knowing what is happening over several days is useful, but does not necessarily affect your intraday trades. Fortunately, moving averages are flexible enough to be used for almost any time period, including intraday.

By the way, when looking at moving averages on an intraday chart, the vocabulary changes slightly. For example, on an intraday chart you will look at a 20-period moving average or a 50-period average (and not a 20-day or 50-day average on a daily chart). I mention this because many traders are not aware of this. In other words, a 50-period or 200-period moving average refers to an intraday chart. However, intraday charts have time frames such as a 5-minute, 15-minute or 60-minute period. Therefore, in a 5-minute chart, each candle, bar or period represents 5 minutes. In a 60-minute chart, each candle, bar or period represents 60 minutes. Another treat: A 10-period moving average on a 10-minute chart uses 100 minutes of price action in total to calculate the moving average. All day traders have their preferred time frames, but on a 60-minute chart the 65-period and 135-period are popular.

Exponential Moving Average

For more accurate information, consider using exponential moving averages, which are calculated in the same way as simple moving averages, but give more weight to recent periods.

Moving average experts point out that while the simple moving average is useful, it can be somewhat slow to respond to market changes. Thus, when faced with the choice between the simple and exponential averages, many traders choose the exponential average.

The use of moving averages

It is often useful to take a step back and use moving averages to look at the market from a long-term perspective.

If a stock crosses the 200-day moving average in one direction or the other, it is more than likely to react. The same applies to the 20-day MA and the 50-day MA.

A large number of traders are watching these large moving averages, and this is something you can do. As you see more and more of the crossover, you can record the data in your trading sheet, and eventually you may have enough information to decide whether this crossover is a tradable signal for you.

Die "Moving average crossover"-Strategie

However, as a daytrader your overall picture will be much shorter. For example, if the stock price crosses below the 5-period, 10-period or 20-period moving average on an intraday chart, this is a negative signal.

Finally, moving averages act as support and resistance, so a cross above or below the moving average is a signal you should not ignore. Other traders use the 30-period or 200-period period on an intraday chart, such as a 30-minute or 60-minute chart.

A popular longer-term signal: when the 8-day moving average (the shorter moving average) crosses above the 13-day moving average (the longer moving average), this might be a buy signal. Conversely, when the 8-day moving average (the shorter moving average) crosses below the 13-day moving average (the longer moving average), this could be a sell signal.

Again, day traders use intraday charts such as the 60 minute, 15 minute and 5 minute charts for signals, not the daily chart. Although moving averages are useful, they are not perfect. First of all, they are called "lag indicators" because they sometimes give late signals. By the time you notice the signal, the buildup is over. Also, moving averages work well when a stock is in a trend, but when the stock is in a trading range (unsettled and trendless), moving averages do not seem to work so well. Even with these limitations, moving averages are signals that should not be ignored, and most day traders study them closely.

Bring the sliding averages to a higher level: MACD

Convergence Divergence (MACD), a technical indicator popular with many traders, also helps to identify when trends might begin or end.

The MACD was created in 1976 by Gerald Appel and consists of two lines, a solid black line called the MACD line and a dotted red (or grey) line called the 9-day signal line, which is actually a moving average of a moving average.

The MACD line is the faster of the two lines (the shorter the time span, the faster the line). The key to understanding MACD is to observe how the faster MACD line interacts with the slower signal line. (If you are interested: MACD is the difference between the exponential moving 12- and 26-day averages. The signal line is the exponential moving average of MACD). The MACD generates a series of signals that traders look for.

For example, when the MACD crosses the 9-day signal line, this can be a buy signal. And when the MACD crosses below the 9-day signal line, this can be a sell signal. You will also see a flat horizontal centerline, the "zero" line. When the MACD crosses above the zero line, this could be a buy signal. Conversely, when the MACD crosses below the zero line, this could be a sell signal. If you have never used technical indicators before, you may wonder how they work.

The answer lies in the formula, which can become complicated. The MACD is, as already mentioned, a calculation of the difference between the closing prices of two exponential moving averages. The result is displayed on a chart next to a moving average of the difference. Since the MACD is such a flexible indicator, you can choose between different settings. Although the default settings are 12, 26 and 9 (12-day exponential moving average, 26-day exponential moving average and 9-day signal line), as a day trader you will use much shorter signals. Nonetheless, you may want to look at the MACD over multiple time periods, such as daily and weekly charts, to get an overview of the overall picture. Consider experimenting with a setting of 6, 19 and 9, as suggested by Appel in his book "Power Tools for Active Investors". Appel also says that traders should pay special attention when the MACD crosses the zero line because he believes that this signal has a better chance of being correct.

For example, if the MACD crosses the zero line, this can be a buy signal. When the MACD crosses below the zero line, this could be a sell signal. Why can't I give you a more definitive answer? First, no indicator is perfect and there is always the possibility of false signals. Second, you do not want to take a large position based on the results of an indicator.

Instead, many traders use indicators to confirm what they already see on a chart. The signal helps them to make a decision. Another signal to look for is divergence, for example, when the price moves up but the MACD moves down, and vice versa. Many traders look for signs of divergence in MACD and believe that this can lead to profitable trading. In addition, many traders rely on the MACD histogram developed by Thomas Aspray. A histogram is plotted above the MACD to provide a visual representation of price dynamics (e.g. the speed of rising or falling stock prices). If the "peaks and valleys" of the histogram become smaller, this means that the dynamics are slowing down, which may signal a change in direction.

Conversely, as the "peaks and valleys" become higher and lower, this may mean that the dynamics are decreasing, which may signal a change in direction. To fully capture the MACD, you must take the time to experiment with the settings.

If you decide to use this indicator, you will probably use several time frames with different settings. The MACD can be used for very short-term charts (e.g. 5-minute, 15-minute and 60-minute charts) up to daily, weekly or monthly charts.

CHAPTER 5: What it's really like to be a daytrader

These chapters I would like to share with you in the form of a story. You can expect a short story about Martin and Richard and how you can avoid drastic mistakes through their story and bad examples.

One thing you should know when you become a new dealer: You will lose money. That's right, on a typical day or week, you will probably lose more trades than you win. This is the price you pay as a newcomer.

I know that some new traders are entering the market and already expect to earn 200€ or 500€ every week or every day. I am here to tell you that this is simply not a realistic goal. If you can earn 20 percent in a year, you will beat the vast majority of professional traders. In fact, it would be fantastic if after the first year you still have enough money to continue trading. By then you will have a PhD in mistakes, the degree that almost every trader earns in the first year. From now on, I will take you into the trenches with day traders so that you can learn how to use all these tools to make profitable trades.

Short story: A bad trade

Since I wanted to be different from other authors, I decided to give you a realistic idea of what it is like to make a really bad trade.

If I simply listed the rules, as most authors do, you would not learn what it is really like to be an undisciplined trader. Therefore, I have written this chapter as a narrative based on a largely true story of an inexperienced trader. Unfortunately, thousands of other traders have had similar experiences at some point. I hope that by reading about his mistakes you can avoid repeating them. In reality, most traders have to learn the hard lessons for themselves. **My goal is to save you from such experiences.**

The Tip

At work, Martin got into conversation with a regular customer, Richard (not his real name), who seemed to have a lot of money.

Richard drove a nice car and had a condo by the sea. Richard told Martin that he made a really good living from stock trading. "I trade stocks for a living," Richard explained. "I am a professional day trader."

The stock market had been on the upswing for several years, but had been extremely volatile in recent months. For many traders this seemed to be a good time to make bargains. Martin had his eye on a low priced share, which he could get for only 7€ per share. He immediately told Richard about his idea. "Stay away from such shares," said Richard. "They have no volume and a bad history." Martin was eager to participate in the market. "So what do you recommend?" "I belong to a group of professional traders," said Richard, "but first you must promise not to tell anyone about my trades.

"I promise," said Martin. "Okay, we really like the City Group for a position trade," he said almost in a whisper, "but first you have to promise not to tell anyone about my business. "It was trading at €50 per share, but now it's €38. We think this is a good buying opportunity". Martin was impressed by the Stadtgruppe, one of the most famous banks in the country. Martin went on the internet and researched what other analysts think about this company. The consensus seemed to be positive. Everyone liked it. "How many shares should I buy?" Martin asked. "That's up to you," said Richard. "I bought 4,000 shares for my account." 4,000 shares! That would cost Martin 152,000 euros, an impossible sum to receive. "What if I had bought 1,000 shares?" Martin asked. "This is a good start," replied Richard. "We expect it to drop back to €50 per share in the near future." That would be a gain of 12 points! Martin enjoyed the idea of earning €12,000 in a few weeks.

He could never earn that much money by waiting on the tables. Martin was tired of being a waiter and was eager to make a fortune on the stock market.

Since he worked at night, he could act during the day and still come to work before his night shift began. Martin's biggest problem was funding his account. He had already saved 5,000 euros, but he needed much more money to buy 1,000 shares at 38 euros. First he charged his credit card with 5,000 Euros. Then he begged his parents for money, but his father had a better idea. He agreed to add Martin to his trading account as long as Martin shared the profit. The two men went to the brokerage firm and signed the necessary application forms.

The ascent

Martin placed his first trade at 9:40 am, ten minutes after the market opened. He entered a market order for 1,000 shares while Coca-Cola continued to move.

He bought 1,000 shares at €40.50. Cost: €40,500. Initially, Coca-Cola increased its stake by two further points to €42.08, which earned Martin an unrealized profit of over €1,500. That was more money than he ever earned in a day as a waiter. He considered selling, but he wanted a home run, not a single one. "To make a lot of money, you have to bet a lot of money," he told himself.

When the market closed that day, Martin decided to hold the share overnight and was thrilled that he had still made a profit of 1,500 euros in one day. That night, Martin's confidence in Coca-Cola grew as he read positive articles about the company. A man on television raced over Coca-Cola for more than ten minutes, shouting into the cameras that the stock was a "buy, buy, buy". The only negative articles Martin found concerned the entire financial sector, which seemed to be somewhat weak. But Martin read an article that claimed that Coca-Cola was immune to a possible banking crisis. That evening Martin called his mother and told her that he was going to be rich. His father was also pleased about his son's success. His girlfriend came by to look at his computer monitor. "You should have sold it," she suggested. "I would have taken the money." Martin frowned. "You know nothing about the stock market."

Market chaos

In the following weeks, the market fell by more than 1 percent, as did Coca-Cola. In fact, Coca-Cola fell by 7 points (more than 15 percent) to around 35 euros.

His profit of 1,500 euros had turned into a loss of 5,000 euros. He asked Richard for advice. "We will buy more," said

Richard. "Coca Cola hasn't been this low in years. It is too cheap to sell." "I don't know if I can afford to buy more shares", said Martin. "If you don't buy more shares, you are making the biggest financial mistake of your life! yelled Richard into the phone. "Okay, okay," Martin replied, intimidated by Richard's loud voice. So Martin placed another market order for another 1,000 shares. It was executed at a price of approximately €36 per share for a total cost of €36,000. He had now invested over 75,000 € in shares of Coca-Cola.

Over the next few weeks, Martin, like his whole family, became obsessed with Coca Cola. They fired up the stock and nobody could talk about anything else. "When this share rises to 50 euros," Martin promised his girlfriend, "we will have the biggest party ever.

Martin copied the antics of the host of a popular financial program and wrote the stock symbol - C - on each knuckle with a blue marker. Throughout the month, Coca-Cola fluctuated between 35 and 37 euros per share. Martin saw Richard a few times in the restaurant, but there was no news. "Sometimes you just have to wait," said Richard and shrugged his shoulders. Over the next few months, the stock market fell by more than 3 percent, but Coca-Cola fared even worse, falling to 25 euros. When Martin looked at the computer screen, he became dizzy. Now he and his father had fallen over 25,000 euros. "I can't believe it," Martin groaned. He called Richard, who told him that what was happening in the market was an unusual event. "You can't plan for the unexpected," he told him. "Just wait and see. It will come back." Martin hoped he could make up for it.

He wanted his money back. A few months later, Coca-Cola dropped another 5 points. Martin had more than 37,000 euros in losses and now owed the brokerage firm the margin he used. Martin kept calling Richard, but there was no answer. Finally, he reached him one late evening. " Richard, what should we do with Coca-Cola? The price is 20 euros per share. I will be killed". "Oh, Coca-Cola. I sold this share a month ago", Richard flipped out. "And never call me again!" Late that night, Martin received a call from his father.

"I got a margin call from the broker this afternoon," he said. "I have to add more money within twenty-four hours or they will sell all the stock. I feel sick." Martin felt even worse. The next morning, Martin hoped Coca-Cola would recover, but it went further down. His father called Martin. "I sold it," he said. "We were cheated with the stock." When the position was liquidated with commissions and fees, Martin and his father had lost over 45,000 euros. Martin personally owed 10,000 euros in credit card fees.

Lessons learned

Later that evening, Martin sat down and wrote down all the mistakes he and his father had made at Coca-Cola. He was shocked at what he had done. "How could I be so stupid?" he thought.

What went wrong: 33 lessons

Ironically, most of Martin's worst mistakes happened before he made his first trade.

The first financial mistake Martin made was buying a share based on a tip, even from a so-called financial professional like Richard. Martin thought that Richard was smarter than the market, a fatal mistake. Tipsters like Richard are everywhere, and it costs them nothing to give free advice. The only antidote to listening to stock tips from so-called trading experts is to close your ears and not pay attention.

Lesson #1: Do not listen to tips.

Martin borrowed money from his credit card to fund his account - a serious money management mistake.

Even with his father's help, Martin was trading with money he could not afford to lose, which should have forced him to be especially careful. Instead, he took unnecessary risks. The pressure to pay back his family and make a big deal was enormous. The professionals call this trade "scared money".

Lesson #2: Don't borrow money to fund an account and under no circumstances take additional risks.

Martin believed that to make a lot of money he had to bet a lot of money.

This myth is perpetuated to separate people from their money. Martin should have invested a small amount of money, especially when he started as a trader. He did not expect that if you bet big, you can lose big.

Lesson #3: Careful with money.

Be aware of how much money can be lost and be sure that you can afford to lose it. Based on the advice he heard from Richard, Martin entered the market with unrealistically high expectations.

For example, Richard Martin lured people into the trade by saying that Coca-Cola "should be at 50 euros per share". The market doesn't care what Richard or anyone else thinks. There is no "should" when it comes to the market; anything is possible. As Martin learned the hard way, the market always has the last word.

Lesson #4: The market is always right.

Martin expected huge profits for this trade.

Yes, it is true that Martin "could have" made profits of 10,000 euros or more, but he also did not foresee potential losses. He also assumed that he could earn 50,000 Euros each year by trading shares. Unfortunately, he did not consider any of the loss days.

Lesson #5: Enter the market with realistic expectations and do not expect fake profits.

These errors could have been avoided if Martin had prepared a set of rules and a trading plan before entering the market.

The rules should have been posted clearly visible: an entry price, an exit price and a stop loss. Since Martin had no rules, he ended up making impulsive trades without having any idea what he was doing.

Lesson #6: Create a trading plan and follow rules.

Instead of asking: "How much can I earn?" Martin Richard should have asked immediately: "How much can I lose?

This would have forced Martin to use "stop losses" and take other steps to protect his client. If he had been more knowledgeable, he could have set price warnings. Martin traded over 75,000 euros and did not plan a "worst case scenario".

Lesson #7: Use Stop Losses or Price Warnings

Martin should also have followed a basic rule of money management: Do not risk more than a certain amount of your total account when you trade.

For example, some retailers will not risk more than 2 percent of their portfolio. However, 2 percent may not be realistic for day traders in retail. The "2 percent rule" is a useful guideline, but it is not set in stone. With a little experience, however, you can set your own percentage.

Unfortunately, Martin did not know that he should decide in advance how much he should risk on his total account until it was too late. For example, if he had only risked 500 shares and included a "stop loss", Martin would have been protected.

Lesson #8: Set a "Stop Loss" and do not risk more than a pre-determined amount on each individual trade.

Perhaps Martin's biggest mistake was to think that his secret weapon Richard would keep him out of trouble.

Because Martin thought that this was a risk-free trade, he took incredibly big risks.

Lesson #9: There is no such thing as a risk-free trade.

When Martin began to think about all the money he could "earn", greed clouded his judgment.

It is not surprising what happened to Martin. As he learned the hard way, ignorance combined with unrealistic expectations and greed can do strange things to people. Remember: As a daytrader you must take what the market gives you, not what you think you deserve.

Lesson #10: Have appropriate goals and post gains when goals are achieved.

Amazingly, all these mistakes were made before Martin even placed his first trade.

He was doomed from the start, but he also made some mistakes in placing orders. For example, Martin bought Coca-Cola on the open market. Since the shares occasionally have a gap in the first trade of the day, entering orders at this time can often lead to poor fills. It is better to wait at least fifteen minutes before placing a trade, especially if you are a newbie. You have all day to trade, so be patient.

Lesson #11: Avoid trading during the first fifteen minutes after market opening.

Another warning sign that Martin ignored was the excitement he felt when he placed his first trade.

"The trade should be as emotional as dropping off the laundry at the dry cleaner's," quipped one professional trader. But you deserve to be satisfied if you look at a profitable monthly or quarterly return.

Lesson #12: Learn how to act without emotions

Unfortunately, Martin was so eager to buy Coca-Cola that he entered a market order, which resulted in a particularly poor execution.

In this trade alone, he lost over one point per share, which cost him more than 1,000 euros. Martin should have set a limit and taken control of the trade and told the market the price he was willing to pay. Instead, Martin rushed into the trade without thinking and let the market decide the price.

Lesson #13: The market is like an auction; use limits to get a more competitive price.

In addition to using limits, Martin could have entered trading with a hundred shares.

Scaling can be an effective way to test the market environment. Although Coca-Cola initially rose, the decline the next day was a warning sign. Martin would have been wise to start with fewer shares. Trading 1,000 shares at once was risky.

Lesson #14: Consider entering into a trade with fewer shares.

Finally, Martin was doomed to failure because he was unfortunately not prepared for psychological warfare.

When Martin came to the market, he traded with sharks, and he was the fish buddy. Reading some books and financial newspapers about the market did not prepare him for the financial struggle of his life.

If anything, Martin should have spent weeks, if not months, practicing and preparing for his first trade.

Lesson #15: Prepare in advance before you place your first trade. Practice trading.

Martin made more mistakes after the purchase of Coca-Cola. First he increased by 2 points. He didn't realize that the management of profit stocks is often as challenging as dealing with loss-making stocks.

The most important goal for a trader is to manage risk so that losses do not become too great. Although blinded by his 2-point gain, Martin should have set a "trailing stop loss" due to the higher price.

Martin also bragged to his parents and girlfriend about his trading skills, a flashing red warning signal. The feeling of earning 1,500 euros within minutes was intoxicating, but also dangerous for his portfolio. After earning so much money, Martin was tempted to believe that trading was easy.

Lesson #16: Avoid greed by using "Stop Losses".

In fact, Martin was so pleased with his so-called tradability that at some point he left the house and put his account on autopilot.

It is known from some inexperienced traders that after placing a trade, they go on a longer vacation and then return to an almost empty account.

Lesson #17: Never let an active trade out of your sight.

A blatant psychological sell signal flashed up when Martin wrote the letter C on his knuckles.

After Martin had fallen in love with this share, he lost all objectivity. He stopped paying attention to negative newspaper articles and only listening to people who supported his view.

With so much money at stake, Martin should have closely monitored the market using technical indicators. When Martin became the company's cheerleader, it was too painful to sell. Instead of relying on the facts in his trading decisions, he relied on hope and Richard.

Lesson #18: Don't fall in love with a stock.

Since Martin no longer had a neutral view of the share, he did not prepare for a "worst case scenario". Simply put, he had no idea what to do if he or Richard was wrong.

Some traders assume that a stock is a turkey until proven otherwise.

For Martin it was inconceivable that the share of such a well-known and powerful company could crash. As a result, Martin continued to watch helplessly without entering into a "stop loss". If he had done so, his portfolio could have been saved and the damage might have been minimal.

Lesson #19: Plan for the worst case scenario by using "Stop Loss Orders".

When the stock recovered on the first day, Martin stopped paying attention to the overall market and the sector of Coca-Cola, the financial stocks. If Martin had looked, he would have noticed that both had problems.

Lesson #20: Examine the overall market and each sector for clues.

Had Martin studied the market, he might have noticed that several key indicators, such as moving averages, gave warning signals.

For example, Coca-Cola and the entire stock market traded well below its 200-day and 100-day moving averages, a big warning signal. Nor was it the smartest decision to bet on rising prices in a potential bear market. The only indicator Martin followed was Richard, a catastrophic mistake.

Lesson #21: Use technical indicators.

When Coca-Cola fell by 5 points, Martin panicked. Instead of pulling out with a relatively small loss, he made a terrible mistake: he bought more shares and doubled his loss position.

Due to a series of emotions, inexperience and bad advice, Martin now risked a financial Armageddon. An experienced trader would have accepted the loss and looked for other possibilities. Martin, however, could not let go.

Lesson #22: One must be prepared to accept some losses.

Although many traders can handle winners, they often have no idea what to do with losers.

The pressure on Martin to be successful as a trader was overwhelming, not only financially but also emotionally. The loss of money, which represented all his hopes, dreams and self-esteem, caused Martin to make impulsive decisions.

When the stock did not perform as expected, he should have reassessed the trade and pulled out immediately. In Martin's opinion, this one bad trade had to be successful, otherwise he would lose the respect of his family, the love of his girlfriend and his self-esteem. It was not surprising that he reacted anxiously if the stock did not perform as expected.

Lesson #23: Learn how to lose before you win

Another big mistake Martin made was overtrading.

When Coca-Cola no longer went his way, he acted again instead of leaving the position in peace. The best traders wait patiently for other, more profitable stocks. Martin was so intent on recouping losses that he made a so-called revenge trade.

Lesson #24: Be patient and wait for profitable trading opportunities

Perhaps the most dangerous mistake of all was Martin's abuse of the margin.

With the help of his father, his account was increased to 100,000 euros. Martin and his father were emotionally unprepared to handle so much money.

They did not understand how a leverage effect increases losses on the way down. In the hands of an experienced trader, leverage can be a very powerful tool. In the hands of an inexperienced trader like Martin, it can wipe out an account.

Lesson #25: Newcomers should avoid using margin.

Another mistake Martin made was to change his strategy from a trade to an investment.

When the price of Coca-Cola fell, instead of immediately selling for a relatively small loss, he waited for the share to return to a balanced level.

Moreover, he should not have taken the position home once the stock went against him. After Martin's original plan failed and the losses multiplied, a complete exit was the only solution.

Lesson #26: Reduce your losses at a predetermined price and sell when the original plan no longer works.

If Martin had spent as much time thinking about a sale as he did about a purchase, he might have made a profit from this trade.

Martin had no idea when to sell and was too inexperienced to realize that 2 points was the highest the market would ever give him in this trade. (Even if he was selling at a profit, Martin, as an amateur, could have complained that he "could, could, and should have made more money from the trade. This is another reason why he needed a "trailing stop").

Lesson #27: Have a sales plan before you buy.

In fact, Martin's only sales plan is to wait for Richard to tell him what to do.

By relying blindly on Richard for all trading decisions, Martin traded for only one day. If he had learned how to find his own shares and make his own decisions, he could have traded for a lifetime.

Lesson #28: Think for yourself.

Even more dangerous for Martin's trading account and his self-esteem was that Martin allowed Richard to bully him and yell at him to buy a share.

If someone yells at you to buy or sell a stock, it might be better to do the opposite. At least Martin should have taken the time to study and think, but he was too emotionally involved. Martin could have obtained a second opinion from a trustworthy professional. However, as it turned out, Richard was not interested in Martin or how much money he was making or losing.

Lesson #29: Don't let anyone push you into a deal.

Martin's merit was that he finally sold. He realized how ridiculously risky the deal was and got out before his father's account was completely destroyed.

It could have actually been much worse. In the course of the next few months, Coca-Cola finally fell below 4 euros per share, where it remained for several years. If the shares of one of the biggest and most powerful banks could lose 90 percent of their value, then you know that anything is possible on the stock exchange. It took Martin years to pay back all the money he borrowed.

Lesson #30: On the stock market, anything is possible.

If Martin had kept a diary of all the mistakes he made in his one bad deal, he could have learned enough lessons for a lifetime.

Since he did not record why and when he bought the share, the number of shares and his price target, he acted emotionally. Without the advantage of keeping a diary, he could repeat many of the same mistakes.

Lesson #31: Keep a journal of all trading transactions.

NEVER AGAIN. For months Martin was angry with himself and Richard. "How could I have been so stupid," he said to himself repeatedly.

Finally Martin took full responsibility for his bad trade. Had Martin had had more self-confidence and knowledge of the market, he would eventually have ignored Richard's tips and tantrums. A little gossip: Richard never spoke to Martin again. Occasionally Martin saw Richard walking near the bookstore or the shopping center, but Richard quickly ran in the opposite direction and muttered to himself: "Uhhhooohhhh, uhhhhhhhhhh". He probably thought that Martin was still angry, but Martin was not angry at all.

They never spoke to each other again, but that didn't matter. The lessons Martin had learned from this one bad trade helped him not only in the stock market but also in life. In retrospect, many of Martin's trading mistakes were due to low self-esteem, insufficient knowledge and inexperience. Most importantly, Martin learned to trust his own judgment when it came to the stock market or making a decision. It is sensible to listen to other people but not to rely on them when it comes to the final decision. Many traders do not know what they are talking about.

Lesson #32: Trust yourself.

Even after losing so much money, Martin did not give up. The next year he studied the stock market diligently and became much more knowledgeable.

After paying back what he owes to his family, he plans to get back into the market, slowly and carefully and with much less money.

"I will not make the same mistakes," he wrote in his diary. He paid a high price, but ironically the lessons he learned from a bad deal were the best thing that ever happened to him.

Lesson #33: Turning lemons into lemonade.

I hope this story has given you some insight into how inexperienced traders can lose their entire portfolio in a single bad trade. As you can see, trading is an incredibly emotional experience, much like a roller coaster ride with your pockets full of cash. As a day trader it can be even more intense.

As I said before, your first goal is to learn how to be a good trader, not necessarily to make money. The most important thing is that you always take steps to protect your portfolio: Preserving your capital is your primary goal. There will always be more trading opportunities, but only as long as you can stay in the game.

After a few months of trading, you will have a much better idea of whether trading is right for you. As you now know, successful trading means mastering money and emotions. If you are not able to control both, then you might want to reconsider whether you should continue trading. Although the mechanisms of action are relatively easy to learn, it is a great challenge to make lightning-fast decisions while juggling thousands of dollars. Rather love what you do or look for another way to make a living.

Closing words

Now that you have a better idea of what it means to be a daytrader, it is up to you to decide what to do next. You can continue to learn and research and follow my advice to practice trading before you put real money on the market. Or you can open your first trading account. Either way, one of my goals was to prepare you emotionally for a tough fight.

Think about further education in the future. There will always be something new to learn: new technologies, new strategies and new software. As the market changes over time and new rules are added or removed, there will always be opportunities to make money for those who are informed and alert.

I would like to thank you for taking the time to read my book. If I could help you to earn or save money, I would be very happy. The most important thing for me is that I hope that I have motivated you to learn more about the stock market.

I wish you all the best!

Disclaimer

The implementation of all information, instructions and strategies contained in this (e-)book is at your own risk. The author cannot accept liability for any damages of any kind for any legal reason. Liability claims against the author for material or immaterial damages caused by the use or non-use of the information or by the use of incorrect and/or incomplete information are excluded in principle. Therefore, any legal and damage claims are also excluded. This work was compiled and written down with the greatest care and to the best of our knowledge. However, the author accepts no responsibility for the topicality, completeness and quality of the information. Printing errors and misinformation cannot be completely excluded. No legal responsibility or liability of any kind can be assumed for incorrect information provided by the author.

Copyright

Imprint

Printed in Great Britain
by Amazon

74909814R00058